Really Useful Guides

John

The Bible Reading Fellowship
15 The Chambers, Vineyard
Abingdon OX14 3FE
brf.org.uk

The Bible Reading Fellowship (BRF) is a Registered Charity (233280)

ISBN 978 0 85746 751 5
First published 2019
10 9 8 7 6 5 4 3 2 1 0
All rights reserved

Acknowledgements

Scripture quotations are taken from The Holy Bible, New
International Version (Anglicised edition) copyright © 1979, 1984,
2011 by Biblica. Used by permission of Hodder & Stoughton
Publishers, a Hachette UK company. All rights reserved. 'NIV' is a
registered trademark of Biblica. UK trademark number 1448790.

Every effort has been made to trace and contact copyright owners
for material used in this resource. We apologise for any inadvertent
omissions or errors, and would ask those concerned to contact us so
that full acknowledgement can be made in the future.

A catalogue record for this book is available from the British Library

Printed and bound in the UK by Zenith Media NP4 0DQ

Really Useful Guides

John

Robert Willoughby

Series editor: Derek Tidball

Each Really Useful Guide focuses on a specific biblical book, making it come to life for the reader, enabling them to understand the message and to apply its truth to today's circumstances. Though not a commentary, it gives valuable insight into the book's message. Though not an introduction, it summarises the important aspects of the book to aid reading and application.

This Really Useful Guide to John will transform your understanding of the biblical text, and will help you to engage with the message in new ways today, giving confidence in the Bible and increasing faith in God.

Contents

Foreword

Robert Willoughby taught New Testament and political theology at London School of Theology (LST) from 1984 to 2015. He loved teaching, encouraging students to be curious, to think boldly and expansively, to grow in their faith in and love for God. The lecture room, the seminar room or conversations over lunch all provided opportunities for discussion.

One student from the '90s wrote:

As I think of Robert, I think of John, the disciple whom Jesus loved. Robert helped me and other students to understand and appreciate John's gospel. The content and tone of his lectures and life have left a lasting impression. It was clear that Robert was not only a disciple whom Jesus loved, but a disciple who loved Jesus and whose students loved him.

John's gospel was Robert's favourite book in the whole world.

Throughout his ministry at LST, he regularly preached to wider congregations who appreciated his ability to place complex truths in their grasp. More recently, he preached very regularly, after being ordained and serving as a priest in St Michael's Highgate. He was a teacher and pastor. He loved to preach from John.

Some years ago, Robert introduced a sermon on John 14:1–17 by reflecting on what people might leave behind, as a last will and testament. Robert treasured his father's copy of *Tom Brown's Schooldays*. John Wesley apparently left a cloak, a Bible and a silver spoon. Jesus left a seamless cloak. But all three left behind far more than just material things, overwhelmingly so in the case of Jesus. Robert reminded his listeners that people who are grieving the death of a loved one, unconcerned about material goods, will often simply say, 'I just didn't want *you* to go. It's *you* that I want!' Jesus' disciples could not conceive of life without him. In John 14, Jesus was preparing them for his departure. He promised he would not leave them as orphans. He gave them hope. This was part of his last will and testament.

Robert died very unexpectedly in September 2018. He had just completed the text of this book. It is the distillation of 40 years of reflection and delight in John's gospel. He wanted his readers to share his enthusiasm and to burrow their way deeper into the gospel.

As a family, Mark, Louisa and I would loudly echo the words of Robert's sermon – 'We just did not want *you* to go. It's *you* that we want!' But Robert's life on this earth is over. He has completed what God had called him to be and to do. On the resurrection day, he will join with Christ and all the saints (which includes us, family, friends, colleagues and LST students over the years, all with our resurrection bodies) in the new creation, the new heaven and new earth.

This book, as it explores the gospel of John, is part of the last will and testament of Robert Frank Willoughby!

Ro Willoughby

Introduction

Dear Reader

John is my favourite book. Not just in the New Testament, nor even in the Bible – but my favourite book. Full stop. Over all the years of my conscious Christian life, it has delighted me, puzzled me, comforted me and astonished me. It has raised more questions and caused me to think more deeply and persistently than any other piece of literature. By anyone's measurement, it stands among the truly great achievements of the human spirit and ranks among the greatest literature ever created. I may be exaggerating there, but I don't think so.

So what is it that makes me so enthusiastic about this book, which can be read by many people in its entirety in less than two hours and is just shorter in length than the book you are holding in your hands? There are several reasons, of course, but I'll offer just four.

First must be that it's got the best stories: the wedding feast at Cana, Nicodemus, Jesus meeting the Samaritan woman, the man born blind, the raising of

Lazarus, etc. And I'm less than halfway through. These stories are told at length and with significant incidental detail without ever becoming tedious or overlong.

Second, and related to the above, John has some of the most memorable and delightful of characters: they ask questions, have opinions and feelings, and clearly experience the normal reactions to life that we all do. We feel we can know them.

I once asked my daughter, when she was about seven, 'What's your favourite story?' I genuinely was not fishing for a Bible story, but she said, 'Oh, when Lazarus came back to life.' Initially surprised, I asked her, 'So what's your next favourite?' The reply came back: 'The wedding at Cana.' This made me think and I soon realised that, of course, any little girl could easily relate to a sad story of two sisters losing a brother and having things put right by this wonderful figure of Jesus. And which little girl would fail to warm to a wedding story with a twist? To paraphrase what John says in chapter 1, 'The Word became just like us and lived out his life doing our sort of things. We saw it' (John 1:14).

A third reason is that John's focus is constantly upon Jesus. Like all the gospels, it is not the incidentals that matter but the Master who matters. It is a wonderful portrait of Christ, and it directly draws out his importance and his magnetism without any hesitancy or uncertainty. The reader is overwhelmed by the central character.

Finally, John always deals with important issues. This is always true of the Bible, but that's what makes this book in particular so gripping, for John gets straight to the theological heart of what matters about God sending Jesus. These issues mostly concern our Lord's life and death, but John finds room for many other important issues. The more you read, the more you discover and are astonished by.

My recommendation is that you put down this book right now, turn to John and, if you are able, read it through in its entirety. Try not to stop, even if you don't understand something or are so thrilled that you want to reread a chapter. Just keep on and enjoy the complete story. We'll come back to the whole story in chapter two.

Robert Willoughby

Beginning at the beginning

Do you know the beginning of Stanley Kubrick's 1968 film *2001: A Space Odyssey*? Very dramatically and seriously it opens the film with a shot of the earth from outer space, accompanied by majestic music, and moves to the creation of humanity on the earth. John's gospel has a somewhat similar opening. Its first 18 verses take us outside of time and set the story of Jesus against the backcloth of creation, the story of Israel and the coming of the Messiah.

These verses introduce a great many of the themes that are important as we read the gospel (which are emboldened below). They are poetic and deeply philosophical, take a very broad theological perspective and place the incarnation, as it should be placed, in the context of creation. Indeed, not a few scholars have suggested that the stories of Genesis constitute an essential background to reading John.

In the beginning was the Word, and the Word was with God, and the Word was God. He was with God in the beginning. Through him all things were made; without him nothing was made that has been made.
JOHN 1:1–3

In the first five verses Jesus is identified as *logos*, a common Greek word meaning 'word'. Jesus was **God's eternal word**, his active agent by which he created the whole universe. God speaks, communicating through his creation and to it. This is revelation and John is very interested in this theme. People don't always want to hear, which is why John describes how Jesus, the Word, has constant opposition from the Pharisees and those people he simply refers to as 'the Jews' (more of that later). Even his own followers frequently misunderstand him, so he has to try and further explain what he is doing or saying. This often leads to highly ironic situations where we, as readers, understand what is going on, but the people in the gospel do not. Sometimes you even want to laugh, but feel you shouldn't. Indeed, if we had been there, we'd have made the same stupid mistakes. (See Pilate in chapters 18—19.)

Jesus is the source of light and life – themes taken up a number of times in John's account of the life of Jesus. Not for the last time, Jesus is identified as closely as possible with God Almighty, the creator and sustainer of all things. Later in the gospel (8:12), Jesus declares that he is the light of the world, and John follows this up with the wonderful story of the man born blind. He receives his sight – the light – in his healing by Jesus, but the Pharisees, who hate Jesus and the man, reveal themselves as those who are really blind.

In John 1:5 we read, 'The light shines in the darkness, and the darkness has not overcome it.' This is actually a piece of wordplay, a double meaning, which is very typical of John. The Greek word translated 'overcome' by the NIV (and indeed, it can mean that or 'dominated') can also mean 'understood'. So John manages to convey two ideas at one and the same time: that darkness tries but fails both to understand the light and to overcome or suppress it.

Following this majestic opening, John brings us resolutely back to earth, introducing Jesus in relation to John the witness (1:6–9). He is never called 'the Baptist' in John, though we are told that he baptises; nor do we read an account of his baptising Jesus. He is simply a witness who speaks out and identifies the Messiah, but is not in any way to be mistaken for that person himself. So straight away, if we are familiar with the other gospels, if we are observant, we will soon recognise familiar features of the story (in this case, John), but we may also be left puzzled over the unfamiliar treatment in this gospel.

Witness is an important concept that reappears in the story. So also is **world**. Jesus the Word comes into the world that he has made but, ironically, is **rejected** by it – another theme that crops up frequently. Even his own people reject him, though immediately we are encouraged by the thought that those who had **faith** were given power to become children of God (1:10–13). The juxtaposition of 'his own people' and 'children of God' is intentional and at once we encounter one of John's main questions: will Israel, God's people of old, embrace his coming in the person of their Messiah? Some will and some most certainly will not. **A new birth, a new creation**, is needed. John will return to this theme.

The Word became flesh and made his dwelling among us. We have seen his glory, the glory of the one and only Son, who came from the Father, full of grace and truth.
JOHN 1:14

John 1:14 is one of the great verses of the Bible and sums up the incarnation. No wonder John 1:1–14 is habitually read at Christmas in Festivals of Nine Lessons and Carols the world over, usually as a climax of the service. While many pagans in the ancient world might have been able to embrace the message of the first 13 verses of John, verse 14 would act as a terrible shock. God's eternal Word becomes flesh – everything that the surrounding world despised and thought to be unlike God – decaying, sickening, transient and in many other ways bad and contemptible.

But John says that the Word embraced that fate. He 'made his dwelling among us'. John describes the Word, Jesus, making friends and living with ordinary human beings. Not for him the gorgeous palaces and weighted advantages of the rich and powerful. His followers tend to be very ordinary people who have ordinary needs. He has friends and followers to accompany him and '**abide**' with him, that is, they remain with him, stay with him and follow him everywhere.

The phrase 'made his dwelling among us' could be inelegantly translated, 'he pitched his tent/his tabernacle alongside of us'. We saw him, as he did this; we saw **the glory of God, his grace and his truth** – all three crucial concepts that reoccur in this gospel. John remains still rooted in the historical account. John the witness has his say again (1:15) and we are told bluntly that, although God had poured his grace upon Israel in the past by giving them the law, through Jesus his Son truth and revelation were made perfect. This made his followers believe that the Father and Son were as close as possible without confusing them as just one person.

John 1:1–18 is often called the prologue of John (or we might say, the introduction that gets you started), and from verse 19 we step back into a more normal account of the gospel story. Some believe the prologue was written by another hand and is detachable from the gospel itself. It certainly seems to stand a bit apart from what follows. However, it is more reasonable to read it as an introductory poem which sets up what is to follow, placing us outside of time and encouraging us to read the story whole, as we do when we think of someone's life after they have died, understanding each of the parts in the light of the whole. The main difference here is that John's gospel is certainly no obituary, and one of his main messages is that the Jesus we read about is alive and active today.

2

What to look out for

We have already seen that John has his own idiosyncratic way of beginning his gospel, a fresh way of
introducing and speaking about Jesus and a somewhat surprising way of speaking about that important
person whom many of us would think of as 'John the
Baptist'. Here are a few other things to look out for
that are specific to the gospel of John.

The Jews: For most of Christian history, John's gospel
has been thought of as being particularly angled
towards pagan Greek enquirers. The last hundred
years have seen a sea change in that perception.
Nowadays, many readers are struck by the very
Jewish nature of what we read. There is a great deal
about 'the Jews' and much of the gospel is theological
debate between different Jewish groups. We read of
how Jesus fulfils all of the main items of Jewish faith
and practice. He replaces the old wine and the temple
(chapter 2); he brings a new creation (chapter 3); he

extends the boundaries of Israel (chapter 4); he fulfils the main festivals (chapters 5—8); and so on.

The interlocking and interweaving themes: These emerge and subside, only to reappear later like threads on a tapestry – themes such as the Holy Spirit, truth, 'abiding', faith, glory, 'lifting up', witness – sometimes these themes occur principally in what happens and not just in the dialogue.

The number seven: For example, the seven signs, the seven 'I am' sayings and any other multiples of seven you might discover. The narrative is very cleverly constructed to include patterns, sometimes overlying patterns.

Contrasts: John frequently uses contrasting elements, known as dualisms, to express his message, such as light and darkness, truth and lies, life and death, belief and unbelief, knowledge and ignorance.

Deeply ironic situations that occur and reoccur: The central irony is that the creator of the whole world comes to what really belongs to him and is rejected by it. This irony is frequently accompanied by crass misunderstanding. One of the most ironic and culminating points in the gospel is that kings are normally 'lifted up' to be admired and gazed upon, but King Jesus is to be lifted up in shame and agony to be looked at on the cross with his crown on. This is his enthronement, and from here he passes judgement on the spectators. Thrilling or chilling?

Symbolism: John uses symbolism repeatedly, which is not evidence that a saying or an event didn't happen but that the events have a meaning beyond the surface. Take the feeding of the five thousand – in John's gospel it is not just a humanitarian gesture to keep a crowd from starving but hard evidence that God, who is able to feed thousands in the wilderness, is here among us. Similarly, the story of the man born blind is not simply about a man receiving his sight, but a pointer to who really is the light of the world. More or less universal symbols recur throughout John: light, wine, food, darkness, blindness, gardens and so on.

The story: As with any good story, you might like to enjoy the plot and the way that John stretches it out over the first half but speeds it up (while in some ways slowing it down with detail) in the second half. Or you might like to enjoy how he links stories up by themes and recurring patterns.

Any good story has great characters. If you find many of the subsidiary characters in the other gospels rather flat or two-dimensional, enjoy the complex characters that John includes: Mary and Martha, Mary Magdalene, the man born blind, Thomas, the Samaritan woman, Pilate, Nicodemus, 'the Jews', Nathanael and so on. These are often brief portraits, but very memorable ones.

3

Puzzling things about John

When was John written?

When might this gospel have been written, and does being able to date it help in any way to interpret what it says? This is a notoriously difficult issue to pin down, though any writing betrays something of the circumstances in which it was written. However, looking at a document written around 2,000 years ago when we have only a sketchy knowledge of the history of the period, the difficulty becomes very great. External events to help place this piece of literature are very few on the ground.

Nevertheless, this has not discouraged people from making attempts to date John's gospel. Many have assumed that the sophisticated theology of John, and especially the very exalted portrayal of Christ, must mean that it dates from at least the end of the first century, if not the first decades of the second century. But this opinion is based upon the assumption that sophisticated and highly developed theology must take time to develop. That is not always the case. Some very sophisticated delineations of the person of Christ seem to date from a much earlier period in the early church (e.g. Philippians 2:5–11).

One feature of the gospel of John which stands out is the hostility between Jesus and his followers and 'the Jews'. Could this reflect a time in the first century when inter-factional relations were at a real low? This is difficult since relations between followers of Christ and the enemies of Christ were not good at any point in the first or second century. (Generally speaking, such conflict was generated by Jewish people who found it difficult to accept that Jesus might be the long-hoped-for Messiah.)

In the 1970s, scholars began to consider the possibility that, towards the end of the first century, a phrase had entered the Jewish synagogue liturgy that cursed 'Nazarenes', that is, followers of the man from Nazareth and, thereby, sought to exclude them from the worship of the synagogue. This was in turn linked to the rather curious word in Greek implying a similar process within John's gospel: in 9:22 there is the threat that the man born blind might be 'put out of the synagogue'. This word is repeated in 12:42 and 16:2 as a likely eventuality for the disciples.

In subsequent years, this threat of Christians being expelled from the synagogue has been vigorously challenged on the grounds of whether the wording actually meant or implied what was claimed. Undoubtedly, levels of hostility between unbelieving Jews and followers of Jesus is a major component of this gospel. Such hostility was always evident, but it does seem to have become worse at the time of the Jewish–Roman War from AD66 to 70, when the temple in Jerusalem was destroyed by the Romans. Jewish people, whether followers of Christ or not, must have had their loyalties tested. Tensions and bitterness would have been raw, and it is highly likely that they would find expression in the writing of this gospel.

On the other hand, an earlier dating seems possible since there appears to be no suggestion that the destruction of the temple has already taken place, even in 2:13–22 when Jesus clears the temple courts. Perhaps we should date John during that tense period of war before the Romans decisively destroyed it.

All of the above helps us to reflect upon an aspect of reading any text, including John's gospel. A piece of literature tells us not only about the subject under consideration but also about the circumstances of the writer and his or her prospective readers. For example, someone writing about the civil war in England in the mid-17th century might also be expected, in writing about that conflict, to betray concerns and sociopolitical tensions at the time of writing. Likewise, the writer of the gospel of John doubtless betrays a concern for issues that were contemporary and sought to apply what he knew about Jesus in a relevant way, just as a preacher might select and apply a single gospel story to the audience.

This leads us conveniently to our next issue…

Why did John write?

The apparently straightforward answer to this question is simply that he wanted to tell the story of Jesus. This, however, provokes the question: yes, but why did he want to do that? This is an especially good question given that he knows of other accounts that might have served his readers equally well (John 20:30–31; 21:24–25).

The key verses which appear to give us at least part of the answer are:

Jesus performed many other signs in the presence of his disciples, which are not recorded in this book. But these are written that you may believe that Jesus is the Messiah, the Son of God, and that by believing you may have life in his name.
JOHN 20:30–31

A further complication arises, however, with the phrase 'that you may believe'. The ancient manuscripts offer us two different words for 'believe', the difference between them being no more than a single letter. It may be that the earliest Christians were really unsure themselves about which of the two possibilities was most likely.

The first spelling encourages the understanding 'that you come to believe', in which case the purpose of John would be primarily evangelistic, to draw his readers into a faith commitment on the basis of what is written in the gospel. The second spelling would be 'that you continue to believe', in which case the main purpose of the gospel would be pastoral, seeking to confirm believers in what they already believe.

If the main purpose of John is evangelistic, the inevitable question arises as to whom the gospel is primarily aimed at. Some have suggested pagan enquirers, but that would sit oddly with the heavy emphasis upon intra-Jewish discussion and relevance. Pagan readers could hardly be expected to catch the nuances of such issues. But having said that is not to imply that a pagan might not read the gospel, understand enough and turn to Christ, attracted by the fundamentally compelling portrait of Jesus.

Others have suggested that the gospel might have been written to address Jewish enquirers. This suggestion is much more promising as it is concerned with Jesus as a specifically Jewish Messiah. However, this hypothesis struggles to answer why the overall tone is hostile to 'the Jews'. It is true that John contains many examples of Jewish people responding with warmth to the person of Christ, but we cannot ignore the sense that they are the real enemies of Jesus and his disciples.

We are left with the possibility that the writer of John's gospel intended his gospel to address the pastoral needs of Jewish believers who were under pressure to deny their faith and who needed to be confirmed and encouraged, as Thomas is in chapter 20. They faced serious attack, especially at a theological level, to explain exactly why they concluded that Jesus was the long-awaited Messiah. Furthermore, the precise relationship of this presumed Messiah with God the Father must have been at issue, not to mention the experience of the divine Holy Spirit to which later Christians were laying claim.

Who wrote John?

Over the centuries the answer has always been John, the apostle, brother of James. But let us examine this claim a little more closely. Earlier generations were perhaps not so inquisitive or critical about such matters and simply accepted the received wisdom. There is no naming in the original text and the superscription 'According to John' was added much later and hardly provides a ringing endorsement in any case.

The identification is often made with a character in the gospel traditionally identified as the beloved disciple or 'the disciple whom Jesus loved'. The beloved disciple appears clearly in four places in John (13:23–25; 19:26–27; 20:2–9; 21:7, 20–24) and might appear as the unnamed disciple in 1:35–36 and 18:15. He is never actually named, but, of the three main disciples, he can neither be Peter, who is named alongside of him, nor James, who was martyred early on (Acts 12:2). The only plausible candidate is the apostle John.

Other candidates have been canvassed, such as Lazarus, who is specifically referred to as 'the one you love' (11:3), and who certainly has an important place in the gospel. Some have held the opinion that the beloved disciple is simply a symbol of apostolic testimony, with little objective reality in his own right. This seems unlikely, given that this gospel has a real concern for historicity. Thomas also has been strongly defended as a realistic candidate given the climactic nature of his expressed belief at the end of the gospel.

This is the disciple who testifies to these things and who wrote them down. We know that his testimony is true.
JOHN 21:24

One concern is how to interpret the 'we' in this penultimate verse. (See also the 'we' in 1:14.) It may be that what we have evidence of here is subsequent editing or writing up of historical traditions which go back to the beloved disciple, who is the founding father of the community and who may well be the apostle John.

We certainly find strong claims to eyewitness testimony. In John 1:14, the 'we' could simply refer to the church and mean that the apostolic church beheld his glory. However, 1 John 1:1–4 does differentiate between the actual eyewitnesses ('we') and the apostolic church ('you'). In John 19:35, it does seem a somewhat remote way of referring to oneself as an eyewitness, although that could simply be a personal quirk. John 21:24–25 indicates that either the beloved disciple wrote down 'these things' or that he (as the ultimate authority) caused them to be written down by someone else. John frequently adds names (6:7–8; 12:3; 18:10) and vivid details (2:6; 12:3; 18:6; 21:11) where the other gospels omit them. He sometimes even claims to know the inner thoughts of the disciples (4:27; 6:19–21; 12:6).

Community origins?

In recent decades, there has been some support for the understanding that the gospel was the product of a group of churches which held essentially the same theology and that their stories were gathered together to form a coherent account of the life of Jesus. This group is often referred to as the Johannine Community and, while it is difficult to imagine a community producing a single work of such originality and genius as John's gospel, it does have some merit in other regards.

There can be no doubt that, when comparing John with the other gospels, we are reading a very different set of details with a very different slant from them. The great likelihood is that some rough association of churches had their own stories and traced their origins back to a historical witness. Maybe the apostle John was that eyewitness; sometimes he is referred to as the evangelist.

At a later date, the likelihood is that a final editor (or redactor, as that person is usually referred to) gathered together these stories into a coherent narrative and added their own 'brand'. This might explain some of the rather strange incidences of 'we' language throughout the gospel and the sense that more than just one person is involved in the process, as in John 21:24–25:

This is the disciple who testifies to these things and who wrote them down. We know that his testimony is true. Jesus did many other things as well. If every one of them were written down, I suppose that even the whole world would not have room for the books that would be written.

JOHN 21:24–25

4

An overview of the gospel of John

Here is an initial outline of the whole book.

- Introducing Jesus (1:1–51)
- From Cana to Cana (2:1—4:54)
- A tour of the festivals (5:1—8:59)
- Gathering the sheep (9:1—12:50)
- The last supper and Jesus' farewell conversations (13:1—17:26)
- The betrayal, arrest, trial, crucifixion and burial (18:1—19:42)
- The resurrection of Jesus (20)
- The epilogue (21)

5

A more detailed guide to the gospel

Introducing Jesus (1:1–51)

The introduction or prologue (1:1–8)

The story that John tells starts properly at 1:19. But that follows an amazing introduction, usually known as the prologue, in verses 1–18. Looking at it more closely, these opening verses contain information about the identity of Jesus and introduce us to many of the themes that will recur later in the gospel.

Table 1: Titles given to Jesus in the prologue and elsewhere

	Prologue (1:1–18)	Elsewhere in John
1 The logos/Word	1:1–5, 14	
2 The Son	1:14, 18	1:34, 49
3 Christ/Messiah	1:17	1:20, 25, 41

4 The Prophet		1:21, 25, 45
5 Lamb of God		1:29, 36
6 Rabbi		1:38, 49
7 Jesus of Nazareth		1:45
8 The King of Israel		1:49
9 The Son of Man		1:51
10 Holy One of God		6:69

Table 2: Other titles and concepts in the prologue

1 The pre-existent one	1:1–2, 15, 30
2 Incarnation	1:9, 14
3 Agency in creation	1:3, 10
4 The light	1:4–9
5 The life/resurrection	1:4
6 New birth	1:12–13
7 The truth	1:14, 17
8 Fulfilment	1:45
9 Relationship to Father	1:1–2, 18
10 Humanity of Christ	1:14

Table 3: Other motifs in the prologue

1 John (the Baptist)	1:6–8, 15, 19–36
2 Came for the whole world	1:9–13, 16, 27
3 Rejection	1:10–11
4 The world	1:10, 29
5 Glory	1:14
6 Grace	1:14, 16–17
7 Witness	1:7, 15, 19, 32, 34
8 The law	1:17, 45
9 Moses	1:17, 45
10 'The Jews'	1:11, 19
11 The Spirit	1:32–33
12 Faith	1:12
13 Judgement	1:11–12
14 'Greater things'	1:50

The first disciples follow Jesus (1:19–51)

The man identified as a witness rather than 'the Baptist' is approached by priests and Levites who have been sent by Jews from Jerusalem. Straight away, we see that John's main purpose is to point to

Christ and identify him to others. Throughout John's gospel, the Jews are presented as almost uniformly hostile to Jesus. This is something we'll have reason to consider as we follow the story.

John's witness concerns who exactly he is and who Jesus is. Jesus' full identity as God's Messiah is flagged up right from the outset, unlike in the other gospels where there is a level of concealment. John is not recorded as baptising Jesus but twice identifies Jesus as 'the Lamb of God, who takes away the sin of the world' (1:29, 36) – a characteristically fresh and intriguing title.

In the other gospels Jesus calls the first disciples, but John's account is of their approaching him and asking where he is staying. They are invited then to follow him to where he was staying. 'Staying' or 'remaining' (or 'abiding', as the older translations have it) is what followers of Jesus are urged to do. For example, they are urged to 'remain in Jesus [the vine]' (15:4). Once again his identity as Messiah is very clear.

At this point, we read the strange case of Nathanael (1:43–51). The other disciples have urged Nathanael to come over, but he memorably questions whether anything good could 'come from there [Nazareth]'

(1:46). The question is very typical in John. At first it is mildly amusing on an ironic level. We are, after all, considering the one who has already been identified as the Messiah. But it is also deeply theological because Jesus' origins are questioned and affirmed throughout this gospel. In this case, Nathanael knew that the Messiah was to come from Bethlehem (in the south, near Jerusalem), not from Nazareth (up north).

Although Nathanael is an individual, at this point he is made to stand for Israel itself. He is sceptical and questioning. Jesus indeed addresses him, half-humorously, as 'an Israelite in whom there is no deceit', unlike his ancestor Jacob (the first to be called 'Israel'), who is referenced in 1:51 (see Genesis 28:10–16). The fig tree, under which Nathanael was seen sitting by Jesus, is emblematic of Israel at peace. Nathanael quickly believes and declares that Jesus is 'the Son of God; you are the king of Israel!' And, not for the last time, Jesus reflects that there is a lot more to come.

From Cana to Cana (2:1—4:54)

The wedding feast at Cana

If you read chapter 1 carefully, you see that it is laid out in five days (1:19, 29, 35, 43 and possibly 41). Chapter 2 very specifically mentions that the following incident happened 'on the third day': a phrase that, counting the first five days, then three more, means the first day of the week, which resonates for Christians with the day of resurrection. The first readers would be encouraged to read and understand this story in the light of what they already knew about Jesus and his resurrection. It is becoming dense with meaning.

The wedding feast at Cana is about things running out and a brand-new batch being brought into being. It's about new creation; echoes of the old creation, which we observed in the prologue (1:1–18), are clear in the way Jesus addresses his mother as 'woman', as though she were another Eve. Moreover, many Jews expected that when the Messiah came, it would be a time of overflowing wine and abundance. In a classic piece of irony, we read the chief steward saying, 'You have kept the good wine until now.' A funny remark again but with deep theological irony. The story also picks up wedding imagery, with the church as the bride of Christ.

It is often overlooked that in 2:11 this incident is described as Jesus' first sign and that he not only revealed his glory (the presence of God, ultimately revealed in his suffering; see 12:23), but that his disciples began to believe in him. This is messianic glory, not just a magic trick. No wonder the disciples believe!

Seven signs usually identified in John
- The miraculous provision of wine (2:1–11)
- The healing of the official's son (4:46–54)
- The healing at the pool of Bethesda (5:1–15)
- The feeding of the five thousand (6:1–15)
- The walking on the water (6:16–24)
- The healing of the man born blind (9:1–41)
- The raising of Lazarus (11:1–44)

Of course, this misses out the final and greatest of the 'signs', that of the resurrection of Jesus himself in chapter 20. One might also include the haul of fish in chapter 21. When we discover patterns of seven, or any kind of pattern in John, they are frequently not quite so neat or compelling as we might want. They raise questions while fundamentally conforming to a pattern as identified.

From the above list it would seem that 'signs' is simply John's way of referring to miracles, which in Mark are referred to as 'acts of power'. But this would not be completely true. John also refers to the temple cleansing as a 'sign' (2:18) and there is a persistent demand for signs which cannot all be regarded as miraculous. The phrase 'miraculous signs' in some translations of John 2:23 is a classic case of over-interpretation. The original text simply says 'signs'.

Jesus assures Nathanael in 1:50 that he will see 'greater things' (as referred to in 5:20), and later he assures his disciples that the Holy Spirit will perform much greater things through them than even he did (14:12). Not all of these things, or 'signs', can be expected to be miracles. 'Signs' point beyond themselves to the identity of Christ and shed light on who he is. Very frequently they will turn out to be miracles but do not always need to be so.

The cleansing of the temple

The rest of chapter 2 is taken up with John's account of the cleansing of the temple. Although some scholars think this must be a different incident from the one in the other gospels, it seems very likely that it is the same one. John is just not as bothered about chronology and things being in the right order as we are today. Indeed, he seems quite content to emphasise different aspects of a story and tell things in his own idiosyncratic way, for his own purposes.

Like with the preceding story, this account of judgement upon the existing temple in Jerusalem reveals the arrival of something completely new and different as the Messiah comes to his world. Instead of a temple built of stone as a place for humanity to encounter the living God, and which had spent the last 46 years being upgraded, Jesus presents his very own body as the place where humanity will encounter God.

Once again, the Jews fail to understand and make fools of themselves, but John explains how the disciples looked back on incidents like this after the resurrection, remembered what had happened and were able to understand the real theological import of what Jesus had said. Their interpretation was based upon their experience of the risen Christ and shaped by their reading of scripture as it was fulfilled in him.

Nicodemus visits Jesus

Chapter 3, the story of Nicodemus, really begins back in 2:23–25. We are at one of several Passover festivals described in John, and he tells us that Jesus knew how people were beginning to react to him: some with faith on account of his various signs, others more sceptical. But he was wise to the foibles and inconsistencies of fickle humanity.

Immediately following this summing up we encounter Nicodemus, a Jewish leader, a Pharisee. As with many, if not most, characters in John, Nicodemus is also highly symbolic, this time of the nation's religious elite. He comes surrounded by his followers in a kind of symbolic as well as literal night. The darkness represents the spiritual darkness which Nicodemus brings with him.

Is he condescending (3:2)? Or genuinely enquiring? Or does he come as a full-blown sceptic? Jesus certainly ignores the flattery and gets straight to the point, namely the need for a new kind of birth, one that is dependent upon God rather than conferred by birthright or status. Nicodemus now expresses lack of understanding (3:4), which continues until he seems to become totally silent (3:10).

Jesus expresses surprise that one so old and learned doesn't know that God had promised this kind of spiritual renewal to Israel, which entailed cleansing and refreshment. He seems to be alluding to Ezekiel 36:25–28, though there are other Old Testament texts which he might also have had in mind. Once again, new creation is invoked and clearly the time is now. The Messiah is here to bring in this renewal.

It is highly ironic for a Pharisee, a 'teacher of Israel', to be so ignorant of this.

For God so loved the world that he gave his one and only Son, that whoever believes in him shall not perish but have eternal life.
JOHN 3:16

Look who's speaking

From 3:11, something happens which is characteristic of John and tends to puzzle readers. In a world which, unlike today, did not use quotation marks, it is difficult to be sure who is speaking. Is it still Jesus? Is it the writer of the gospel, speaking for himself or even his community of believers (note the 'we' in 3:11)? It's up to the reader to decide. It seems likely that it is Jesus continuing to speak until the end of 3:12. From then on there are no 'I's or 'we's and what we seem to have is a theological reflection on the subject of the encounter between Jesus and Nicodemus, running from 3:13 to 3:21. This climaxes in the great statement in John 3:16, 'For God so loved the world that he gave his one and only Son, that whoever believes in him shall not perish but have eternal life.'

It happens fairly regularly in John that the style of speaking/writing barely differs between that of the writer and what is clearly Jesus himself. This might encourage us to view the gospel as highly reflective and interpretative with the melding together of voices, equally inspired by the Holy Spirit (16:12–15) so that very little distinction can be found between them. The Holy Spirit explicitly brings things to mind and assists in the process of understanding and interpretation (2:22; 12:16; 14:26).

To close chapter 3, John the witness is reintroduced to the narrative for the last time. (He gets one further mention in 5:31–36 to emphasise his inferiority to Jesus.) In 3:22–36, the purpose is to point out that John is being superseded in Jesus. Everyone is now going over to him. And we are told that John is glad about this. 'He must become greater; I must become less' (3:30).

Before we get on to chapter 4 and the Samaritan woman, we should note that the choice whether or not to believe the truth is sharpened for us. Jesus, we are told, is from heaven and speaks the truth; he is, after all, the Messiah, the Anointed One, who 'gives the Spirit without limit' (3:34). The only way to enjoy the benefits of eternal life is to put your faith in him (3:36).

The Samaritan woman at the well

John 4 is one of the longest and best-loved stories in the gospel and, as so often, it is one that only John tells. Jesus has ventured beyond the borders of Israel proper and is going through Samaria. This was unusual for Jews, who would not soil their feet by walking through the country of these 'half-Jews'. The Samaritans were probably the descendants of the racial and religious mixing caused by the transportations and exile conducted by the Assyrians and Babylonians. They were fiercely anti-Jerusalem and had their own traditions concerning the law and messianic hope. Given Jewish qualms about even going there, it is quite astonishing that Jesus should speak to one, and a woman at that, and ask for a drink from one of their wells. Not only is the woman an unclean Samaritan, but, as becomes clear, she also has a rather chequered past!

Numerous theological themes crop up here in the most delightful of stories with the most engaging of protagonists. And, ironically, it's worth comparing this with the stilted and rather unproductive dialogue between Jesus and Nicodemus in the previous chapter. A Samaritan trumps a Jew; a person of low status trumps a leader and teacher; a woman betters a man. And Jesus lets it all happen!

Clearly one of the principal themes here is mission – Jesus transcends boundaries and, in turn, so does the woman, enthusiastically telling her village about Jesus. Salvation may come from the Jews (4:22), but it is not restricted to them, nor is it restricted to the wealthy, the influential or the approved, but fans out to others less fortunate.

Another theme is that of the Spirit's source and role. As they begin to talk about the water in Jacob's (Israel's) well (4:7–15), as in the dialogue with Nicodemus (3:5–10), it becomes clear that, for John, water is closely connected with the Spirit. Getting water out of such a deep well is challenging. Not only that, but it leaves people still wanting more. The old revelation runs dry; it is unsatisfying. Jesus introduces the woman to the idea, which he will return to in chapters 7, 14—16 and 20, that he himself is the source of water (i.e. the Spirit) that is alive and inexhaustible.

Jesus answered, 'Everyone who drinks this water will be thirsty again, but whoever drinks the water I give them will never thirst. Indeed, the water I give them will become in them a spring of water welling up to eternal life.'
JOHN 4:13–14

A further theme is that of revelation. Jesus has been teaching the woman some theology already, but now moves on to her own life. He is the revealer and brings the truth wherever he goes. No wonder this is his food and drink (4:31–38), because that is precisely the role given to the Messiah, of whom Samaritans also had some awareness, though, doubtless, as with everything in their theology, it was incomplete (4:25–26).

Like the disciples in chapter 1, the woman invites her village to 'come, see' (4:29), being another 'witness'. Also like the disciples earlier on, the villagers come and stay, in their case two days. They believe on the basis of their experience. Significantly, they identify Jesus as the Saviour *of the world*.

Jesus heals the official's son

Our second Cana miracle, or sign, closes chapter 4. Once again, it is a story of faith, this time expressed by a royal official's faith in Jesus' ability to heal at a distance. In many ways it resembles the incident of the centurion's servant in Matthew 8:5–13, though there are differences and they should not be confused. However, the themes of Jesus' mission beyond Israel and his power and authority at any distance remain the same. This story forms a wonderful climax to chapters 3 and 4.

A tour of the festivals (5:1—8:59)

The festivals of Israel were key to religious life and practice. Alongside the practice of the law (Torah) and its sense of calling, identity and precise destiny as Israel, festivals bound the people together in worship and recollection of the great factors of their faith. They regularly met up to celebrate together. The nearest we get to this today may be gatherings in large cathedrals or conferences or the Muslim hajj to Mecca. Jews from all over the world would descend at the appropriate time on Jerusalem to celebrate Passover and Tabernacles, filling the temple and the streets with worshippers as well as hucksters (see John 2:13–17; Acts 2:5–13).

Yet the most frequent and fiercely observed is the simplest: the weekly sabbath. This is the underlying festival behind chapter 5. Chapter 6 reflects on Passover and chapters 7 and 8 are shaped by the Feast of Tabernacles.

The sabbath

Sabbath was hardwired into national life as a time, once a week, when most activities simply ceased. But it is also deeply significant theologically, having its roots in the very act of creation as God himself rests in satisfaction at his own act of creation (Genesis 2:1–3). It is also central to the law (Torah) and is elaborated on in a way many of the other commandments are not. It is the fourth of the ten commandments:

Remember the Sabbath day by keeping it holy. Six days you shall labour and do all your work, but the seventh day is a sabbath to the Lord your God. On it you shall not do any work, neither you, nor your son or daughter, nor your male or female servant, nor your animals, nor any foreigner residing in your towns. For in six days the Lord made the heavens and the earth, the sea, and all that is in them, but he rested on the seventh day. Therefore the Lord blessed the Sabbath day and made it holy.

EXODUS 20:8–11

This, of course, also links back to the act of creation, which is important for understanding John 5. We begin with the healing of the man by the pool of Bethesda – the third of Jesus' miracles/signs recorded in John. As the chapter progresses we see clearly, for the first but certainly not the last time, how John elaborates what the particular sign is pointing to. On one level, like all of Jesus' miraculous interventions, it is an act of mercy. The pool area is full of invalids and sick people, many long-term – for this particular man, 38 years! But that is not central to John's account. Only the one man is healed, and his healing is not an act of creation out of nothing, unlike God in Genesis. The man receives the capacity to walk once again.

What really catches the attention of the Jews is that Jesus has done this on the sabbath. There are many healings by Jesus on the sabbath in the gospels, but it is really only John who follows the incident with full-blooded theological reflection. The validity of the healing is in no way under discussion. After all, Israel was familiar with miracle-workers and healers.

An increasingly aggressive dialogue is begun with the Jews, during which Jesus lines up his own behaviour with that of God himself (5:16–18). Now they are not only offended by his breaking the sabbath but also by his 'making himself equal with God'.

What ensues in 5:19–29 is a very strong assertion that Jesus only does, and will continue to do, what he sees his Father doing. Behind the thinking here may be the rabbinic conundrum as to who sustains and upholds the world while God is taking his rest on the sabbath. Of course, the answer must be that God *does* work in some ways on the sabbath and that this healing is another work of God. Indeed, the Father has delegated all of his good work to the Son because of his obedience, including healing and even bigger tasks such as the giving of life and the administration of judgement. Here, we encounter one of those many occasions in John where Jesus identifies himself so closely with God the Father, especially his activity, that it is a very small step to declaring them to be the same. It is surprising, given what happens elsewhere in John, that the Jews make no attempt at this point to lynch Jesus.

The witness theme

John 5:30–47 moves now to the subject already flagged up in 1:7–9, 19–34 and continued by the Samaritan woman in chapter 4 – that of witness or testimony. There is a consciousness that, although Jesus has sufficient stature and authority to make his own claims about himself and his work, the testimony of others is valuable to his listeners or readers.

The first witness mentioned here must overall be God himself (5:32).

The second witness is, unsurprisingly, John the witness (5:32–36), who has been identified already as such. Jesus pays him the greatest respect and points out how fortunate Israel has been to have had him. As John himself affirmed, he was not the light. That, as we shall see in chapter 8, is of course Jesus. But he was a lamp – an instrument whose sole purpose is to hold out a light to be seen by others and by which they also might see.

The third witness is the signs or 'works' (5:36–38), some of which we have already heard of. The Jews had heard of them too, but failed or refused to be guided by them.

The fourth and final witness is the holy scriptures (5:39–47). Jews, especially the Pharisees, loved to study and debate the scriptures, but they absolutely refuse to acknowledge Jesus as the one who is spoken about in them. It is not that they have had no other pointers, for they have seen John and they have seen the signs which also point to him. So, inevitably, Jesus closes the discussion by commenting that it is not he who will finally judge them, but Moses, the archetypal purveyor of law and wisdom.

We have seen how John lines up a variety of witnesses to confirm the identity of Jesus as Messiah:

- God the Father
- John the witness
- The signs/works
- The scriptures

The witness theme runs more generally throughout the gospel. John follows something of the pattern which can be discerned in Isaiah 40—55, where God is depicted as both a judge and a witness over against Israel. One book on John is entitled *Jesus on Trial*.

John lines up his witnesses to point to Jesus and finally sets up the trial narrative with Jesus before Pilate (chapters 18—19). Ironically, Jesus is placed on the judgement seat overlooking the crowd. The main point of this theme is to encourage the reader to decide who Jesus is or to be confirmed in their understanding of his identity.

Passover

These chapters are so self-contained that at least one major commentator has suggested that chapters 5 and 6 could be the other way around. Maybe this is true, but there's no doubt that the Passover festival, which shapes the whole of chapter 6, follows on well from the mention of Moses at the end of chapter 5. And what an appropriate time to take a crowd of people into the wilderness, up a mountain, and teach and feed them miraculously. Passover is our next festival; John 6:4 namechecks it and the abundant grass confirms it is springtime (6:10). As it says in 6:2, the signs Jesus had already performed were directing the crowds to him.

The feeding of the five thousand is one of the few incidents to appear in all four gospels, apart from the events directly leading up to Jesus' death and resurrection. The line of the story is clear enough, though many details are slightly different and John, as so frequently is the case, fills in aspects we don't otherwise know. Characteristically, John begins to draw out the theological significance in a way other gospel writers don't. Observing the twelve basketsful left over, the crowd begins to speculate that this might be the prophet promised in Deuteronomy 18:15–22. Jesus can see where this is all heading. It is not his calling to be a secular-style king, with all that that may entail. He realises this is what they want. It has already been suggested in 1:49 and will be a main theme in his long discourse/trial with Pilate in 18:28–16. So he escapes.

The next incident inevitably calls to mind that other miraculous Passover happening – the miracle of the waters, the parting of the Red Sea. The details here are quite different but, as in the earlier crossing, God is demonstrated as Lord of the waters. Jewish people, unlike the Greeks, were not confident or comfortable in relation to the sea. To them, it was a dangerous place of judgement and death with terrifying monsters in the deep. Jonah's fate had been a truly terrible one, and Jesus' acts of stilling the storm and walking on water were profoundly impressive. It must, however, be the Passover resonances that are uppermost when we read this account.

The crowd and his disciples look for Jesus and find him in Capernaum, puzzled at how he got there. He begins by observing that even the signs don't achieve their proper impact: the crowd follow simply because he meets their needs (6:26–27). Further explanation and discussion must follow. Perversely, the crowd ask for a sign and call to mind the wilderness miracle of manna and quail which their ancestors have enjoyed (Exodus 16). Jesus pushes them spiritually and directs them back to himself with the first of the famous 'I am' sayings found in John.

The 'I am' sayings

These seven sayings, which are nowhere found in the other gospels, clearly recall the self-revelation of God to Moses in Exodus 3:13–15. Here, God reveals that his name is 'I am', which has normally been rendered into English as YHWH or Jehovah, but which no Jew would ever pronounce out of fear and respect. That's why they resorted to calling God 'the Lord'. These sayings also resemble many things said by God in Isaiah 40—55, one of the most majestic portrayals of God's nature in the whole of scripture.

The sayings are:

- I am the bread of life (6:35)
- I am the light of the world (8:12)
- I am the gate (10:7)
- I am the good shepherd (10:11)
- I am the resurrection and the life (11:25)
- I am the way and the truth and the life (14:6)
- I am the true vine (15:1)

Each of these sayings reveals something profound about the identity of Jesus, most specifically about his divine nature. They sum up much of the story which is going on around them and offer a crisp summary of what can be known about him.

Other sayings which resemble them are:

- 'Before Abraham was, I am' (8:58)
- 'I and the Father are one' (10:30)

As chapter 6 goes on, Jesus elaborates the way in which he is the bread of life, teaching which becomes more and more difficult for the Jews to accept. A parting of the ways is pointed out and arrives for many.

Jesus makes many points. First, as we witnessed in chapter 4 with the water which Jesus supplies, he is able to provide real sustenance to anyone who comes to him. Just as the water (of the Spirit) is offered to all, so is the bread. Second, he never turns anyone away who comes to him, continuing the open offer of salvation that John has already identified. Third, this offer constitutes eternal life.

In John 6:41–50, the Jews begin to grumble and complain, which is significantly a repetition of their ancestors' behaviour in the wilderness, when they were confronted by their version of 'heavenly sustenance', the manna and quail (Exodus 16:1–7). Once again, the problem is their inability to perceive the goodness and provision of God and their consequent, terribly unattractive, ingratitude.

Jesus, however, is not finished and raises the stakes further, though it is the Jews who make the leap from discussing him as bread to equating it with his flesh. In 6:51–59, Jesus observes that they must indeed consume his flesh and blood in order to receive the very life that he offers. These are words that might strike anyone as rather demanding, if not disgusting, but, for Jews, who ritually seek to empty meat of any of its blood and who should never eat any blood products, this is unthinkable. The language is extreme and very open to misunderstanding. Right from the beginning, many have found this unacceptable. Pagans, indeed, at the time of the early church ignorantly regarded Christians as cannibals on the grounds that they claimed to eat Christ's flesh and drink his blood.

Understandably, since very early on in Christian history, these words were read as ultimately referencing the supper of the Lord, the Holy Communion. Read in this way, they will certainly draw one to a higher understanding and valuing of that sacrament. Others have resisted that interpretation and understood the bread to be referring to God's wisdom, as one might understand it in Isaiah 55, where the prophet encourages his people to feast on God's words of wisdom. It has to be said that mention of the Word in 1:1 and 1:14 might support such an understanding.

Whichever interpretation we opt for, Jesus' rather extreme demands are too much for some. He has brought them sharply to a point of decision – something which makes John a very potent vehicle for Christian evangelism. In 6:60–71, Jesus and his disciples discuss the difficulties raised by what he has said. Significantly, the text presents the disciples with different responses to Jesus' challenge as to whether they leave or not. Peter's response is, 'Lord, to whom shall we go? You have the words of eternal life. We have come to believe and to know that you are the Holy One of God' (John 6:68–69). But we also notice the reference to Judas which follows.

John and the sacraments

Across the centuries there has been much discussion about John's attitude to the sacraments, especially the universally accepted sacraments of baptism and Holy Communion.

A rather extreme approach manages to see references to the sacraments wherever it is feasible. Thus, it is not just John the witness who early on speaks of baptism, but it is also seen in chapter 3 when Jesus talks about being born 'of water and the Spirit'. The living water mentioned in chapter 4, revisited in chapter 7 and used to wash feet in chapter 13 is seen to be alluding, at least in part, to baptism. The same can be said of Holy Communion, which might be spotted at the wedding feast in Cana in chapter 2, here in chapter 6, at the last supper in chapter 13 and especially in the parable of the vine in chapter 15. And so on. Basically, if you can see any hint of the sacraments at all, it must be there!

A different, but equally extreme, interpretation effectively denies that there are any references at all in John to the sacraments, however surprising that may be. Instead, each of these instances can be understood as using wisdom terminology to elucidate the ministry of Jesus.

As so often, a complex moderating position seems best, where every reader must examine each text in John and decide on the basis of the context whether there is a primary allusion to the sacraments, or even a secondary one. Such close reading is clearly a desirable outcome, though one wonders if final, authoritative conclusions will ever be arrived at.

The Feast of Tabernacles

Tabernacles is the third of our festivals. It is a less well-known festival in the church, as, unlike Passover and Pentecost, we don't really have an equivalent

Christian celebration. But it was very important in Israel's rehearsal of their faith history. It commemorated the itinerant experiences of the people in the wilderness, that most generative experience in their history. (Instructions for its celebration can be found in Exodus 40.) It is connected to the actual tabernacle in which Israel worshipped God until the first temple was built. But it is also associated with the little tents (or booths) in which each Israelite family lived while pursuing their migrant existence in Sinai. They celebrated Tabernacles every year and, just as the Passover was to be eaten quickly to replicate the haste with which Israel escaped from Egypt, so the living in small tents performed a similar function.

John 7 begins with Jesus' brothers urging him to join them in setting out on pilgrimage to celebrate Tabernacles in Jerusalem. John 7:1–9 resumes the sense of hostility and rejection which Jesus has experienced in the previous chapter. There is some discussion as to whether he will go and whether he has arrived, but this is resolved in 7:14–24, when Jesus enters the temple and starts teaching, reviewing many of the themes with which we have become familiar.

Inevitably the question arises as to who this man might be (7:25–36). No one seems to be any the wiser, and both his origins and ultimate destiny are under consideration. Jesus is seriously under threat, and hostile forces such as the Pharisees and the Jews begin to gather forces to arrest him. They have moved on in their hostility since chapter 1.

On the last day of Tabernacles, when water was poured lavishly down the steps of the temple, Jesus speaks up (7:37–52) and develops themes which have been previously aired in 4:13–15. His words echo those of the prophet in Isaiah 55. His invitation, in direct contrast to what is being enacted in connection with the temple, is that he is the source from which they will derive water to drink. In this, he prepares for further teaching, where the reception of the Spirit is described (John 14—16; 20:22).

The Pharisees are unimpressed and begin to accuse those who are of a different persuasion, including one of their own number, whom we met in chapter 3 – Nicodemus. Nicodemus seems be hanging in there, slowly advancing from his tentative appearance and disappearance in chapter 3. Jesus' origins remain an issue. Nicodemus appears again at the burial of Jesus in 19:38–42 with Joseph of Arimathea, where he brings huge quantities of spices for the body. It remains fascinating to consider what this utterly representative Jewish leader really believes at any point in the gospel.

A cuckoo in the nest?

At this point, John presents us with one of the Bible's great conundrums, namely the story of the woman caught in adultery (John 7:53—8:11). The vast majority of the original Greek texts available do not have it, or else they place it at some other point in the gospels. What is clear is that it doesn't belong here. It breaks up the line of the story with its Tabernacles theme and introduces a discussion which is not being had at this point.

However, the style is that of John, and the teaching is clearly that of the New Testament. Both Jesus' actions and his teaching 'fit'. For most people, it has that 'ring of truth'. It is one of the best-known and best-loved stories in scripture.

Most translations of John put it either in parentheses or at the foot of the page, and that seems about the best decision we can arrive at.

The next movement in our story begins with Jesus' second great 'I am' saying and rises to a crescendo with some punishing exchanges between him and the

Jews. 'I am the light of the world,' he declares (8:12). Light, a universal symbol of revelation and insight, conjures up the creation, where it was one of the first things brought into being by God. It provides clarity and insight for discrimination and judgement, especially as to Jesus' origins and identity.

In 8:21–30, we continue to see a clearly deteriorating relationship between Jesus and his opponents, to the point that Jesus wonders why he even bothers to speak with them, perhaps reflecting on casting pearls before swine! He observes that they might understand when he is 'lifted up' (8:28–30) – a rather gruesome phrase, suggestive of a process of not only glorification but also crucifixion. It is John's insight that the two are essentially the same.

The discussion with the Jews reaches its climax in John 8:31–59, and some pretty harsh words are spoken. The discussion again focuses around the question of identity. The Jews/Pharisees declare their pride in being descendants of Abraham, that great hero of faith in God. Jesus insists that that kind of freedom does not absolve them of the capacity to be sinful and, hence, a slave of sin. Freedom from sin only emerges from becoming a follower of and putting one's faith in Jesus (8:31–38).

To the Jews who had believed him, Jesus said, 'If you hold to my teaching, you are really my disciples. Then you will know the truth, and the truth will set you free.'
JOHN 8:31–32

Jesus' rejoinder to claims of descent from Abraham is that they would follow Abraham's example. This evolves into a discussion about legitimacy. His denunciation climaxes with the harsh words:

'You belong to your father, the devil, and you want to carry out your father's desire. He was a murderer from the beginning, not holding to the truth, for there is no truth in him. When he lies, he speaks his native language, for he is a liar and the father of lies.'
JOHN 8:44

The response of the Jews impugns Jesus' own origins, a matter which John has persistently alluded to, and they accuse him of both being a Samaritan and being demonised (8:48). In response, Jesus insists that those who receive his words and the truth that he brings will receive eternal life. This claim riles them further, and they seek to ridicule him for speaking as though he pre-existed Abraham. His reply is that he did, and the inevitable outcome is that they prepare to stone him for blasphemy.

Who are 'the Jews'?

For centuries, Jewish people have complained not only about the clear persecution of them by Christians, but that the impulse towards that is enshrined in the foundation documents of Christian faith – the New Testament. Both Luke and Paul come in for this criticism, but it is Matthew who records the terrible and damning words of the crowd when they choose Barabbas: 'All the people answered, "His blood is on us and on our children!"' (Matthew 27:25).

John, especially in 8:44 quoted above, seems to take the offence a stage further. This is not a charge that the church can take lightly; the history of anti-Semitism is too damning. It is insufficient for Christians to claim that it wasn't us but merely 'nominal' Christians. The charge is that the New Testament encourages it. And here in John, there seems to be no quarter – it is 'the Jews' as such who are demonic and hence damned.

Without wishing to minimise this charge, a number of points need to be made.

1 The term 'Jews' seems to encompass the whole race in John, but that simply cannot be the case. There are significant Gentiles/non-Jews who

appear in John's narrative – the Samaritan woman and possibly the royal official in chapter 4, the Greeks who want to meet Jesus (12:20–21), Pilate at the trial and representative Romans. But every other person in this gospel is a Jew, including most of Jesus' followers – and Jesus himself.

2 The 'Jews' have been variously identified. They may represent the religious establishment which is hostile to Jesus; they may simply refer to Judeans as opposed to Galileans. We cannot be completely sure.

3 The level of antagonism may well be derived from the circumstances prevailing when the gospel was composed. It seems highly likely that the controversies raging about who Jesus was within the first-century Jewish community led to very fierce exchanges and behaviour which are reflected in passages like chapter 8.

4 The heatedness of the language may have been more acceptable in this first-century culture than would be acceptable now.

None of the above removes the problem. Jewish people are likely to find John's gospel provocative. It is for Christians to endeavour to elucidate the probable background to these words, while remaining humble and utterly repentant about two thousand years of anti-Semitism.

Gathering the sheep (9:1—12:50)

The man born blind

Chapter 9 introduces another of the great characters in this gospel – the man born blind. The story opens with a serious theological debate concerning the origins of sickness and other misfortunes. A common position, then as even today, is that the man or his parents must have committed some sin for which God is presently punishing them. Jesus denies this and announces that this man will become a sign for people to understand more about what God is currently doing. He puts mud on the man's eyes and tells him to wash it off at the Pool of Siloam, all the while insisting, as in 8:12, that he is the 'light of the world' (9:5).

The dialogue which ensues is priceless as an example of the ironic way that John tells his story. The man is more than a match for his Pharisaic accusers. Jesus is once again difficult to locate, and once again his background is in question. Who on earth might he be, to be able to perform such a wonderful miracle? The man born blind has been accused of being a sinner and now so, too, is Jesus. The man taunts his accusers and they begin to take steps to throw him and/or his parents out of the synagogue (9:22), thereby not just socially ostracising them but passing theological judgement upon them.

Thrown out but warmly received

The phrase 'put out of the synagogue' (9:22; compare 12:42; 16:2) is one rather unusual word in the original text and has generated a lot of comment in recent decades. Many see this as a reflection of the circumstances prevailing when the gospel was composed – see the earlier discussion on the dating of this gospel starting on page 25. Hostility between groups of Jews who did not have faith in Jesus and those who did, it is speculated, may well have reached the levels of abuse found in the previous chapter. One consequence may have been that Christian Jews were barred from synagogue worship.

There is no cast-iron proof that this is what the story reflects. Maybe this story is being told by John precisely because it resembles some of the cases well known to his Jewish Christian readers who no longer found a welcome from their fellow non-believing Jews.

This story eloquently dramatises the condition of *spiritual* blindness. The irony is exquisite. The man born blind turns out to be very open to the Messiah and his ministry and receives both his spiritual and his physical sight. The Pharisees, who are proud that no one can point to any sin which might explain their blindness, boast that *they*, at least, can see. Jesus makes what is now the obvious point: that their spiritual blindness is particularly intense.

The parables about God gathering his sheep

Chapter 10 introduces one of the two parables in John (the other being the vine in chapter 15). However, if we think of 10:1–18 as just one parable, it will be fiendishly difficult to make sense of it. It is in fact three related parables around the theme of God gathering his sheep, which are stuck together one after another with a great deal of explanation. They are as follows:

1 The parable of evil shepherds (10:1–6)
2 The parable of the gate (10:7–10)
3 The parable of the good shepherd (10:11–18)

The first parable (10:1–6) sets up the reality of thieves and bandits doing harm to the sheep by not approaching them through the ordained channels. Following the events of the previous chapter, John has in mind the Pharisees who want to bypass Jesus in their approach to the sheep. The encouraging aspect is that the sheep recognise the true shepherd and listen only to him. But notice the direction of travel for the sheep. It is easy to misread the text as saying that the shepherd guides them *into* the fold when actually he leads them *out* into open country.

The second parable (10:7–10) identifies Jesus himself as the gate: 'I am the gate for the sheep.' He is the only authentic point of entry. He warns again of thieves and bandits who are looking to do the sheep no good at all. In contrast, he has 'come that they may have life, and have it to the full' (10:10).

The third parable is longer (10:11–18). It begins with another 'I am' saying: 'I am the good shepherd.' The theme of God as the supreme shepherd had a certain pedigree in the Old Testament, especially in Ezekiel 34. Moreover David, as God's servant-king, makes good use of his knowledge and identity as a boyhood shepherd in composing Psalm 23. In claiming to be the good shepherd, Jesus not only contrasts himself with the thieves and bandits but also explicitly assumes a divine role, shepherding God's flock. This good shepherd knows the Father and is recognised by the sheep. He cares for the sheep, whereas the hired hands run away.

Significantly, a new aspect of the shepherd begins to emerge: his laying down his life for them voluntarily, a climax towards which this gospel is hastening. Also hidden away is the observation that there are 'other sheep' who do not belong to this particular fold (10:16). The sense of mission beyond the boundaries of Israel, which we picked up in chapter 4 with the Samaritan woman, re-emerges in a typically subtle and understated fashion.

In 10:19–42, some themes that we have already noticed re-emerge. The hostility of the Jews continues, and their accusation that Jesus is demonised is repeated. They keep pressing Jesus to tell them plainly whether he is the Messiah. Jesus points out that they do not recognise or belong to him, and neither can anyone snatch his true followers out of his hand (10:29). In a climactic provocation, he declares, 'I and the Father are one' (10:30), at which point they attempt once again to stone him, considering this to be a blasphemous statement.

The raising of Lazarus

The raising of Lazarus (11:1–44) is, in many ways, the climax to the first part of John. It is this incident which proves to be the final straw for Jesus' enemies and precipitates events which lead to the cross.

It is a family affair. Two sisters in Bethany, with a dying brother, call for Jesus in great distress. We are told that, although Jesus really loves them, he delays arrival at their house until Lazarus is dead. His delay is to function as a demonstration that his word brings life, even eternal life. As so often happens, what Jesus does is not just out of compassion, but intended as a theological demonstration. When Martha upbraids his tardiness, Jesus declares that Lazarus will rise again.

As a good, faithful Jew, Martha certainly believes her brother will rise again on the last day. That was what a great many Jews believed. Jesus, however, makes a stunning revelation:

Jesus said to her, 'I am the resurrection and the life. The one who believes in me will live, even though they die; and whoever lives by believing in me will never die. Do you believe this?' 'Yes, Lord,' she replied, 'I believe that

you are the Messiah, the Son of God, who is to come into the world.'
JOHN 11:25–27

Note that John includes Martha's statement of faith, which parallels a male disciple's confession in Mark 8:29. As the story progresses, Martha's sister Mary is also very distressed and, in one of the most human moments in all the gospels, we are told that 'Jesus wept' (11:35). Whether he was weeping alongside Mary, weeping at the evident lack of faith or, more theologically, weeping at the universal obscenity of death, we cannot be sure. Perhaps John intends to imply all three.

The climax of the story is spine-tingling as Jesus calls out Lazarus from the tomb, still bound by his grave clothes.

Some Jews begin to believe; others fear that such events will destabilise the fragile status quo and incur the wrath of the Romans. It is at this point that Caiaphas, the high priest, delivers this chilling but profoundly accurate prophecy:

Caiaphas, who was high priest that year, spoke up, 'You know nothing at all! You do not realise that it is better

for you that one man die for the people than that the
whole nation perish.' He did not say this on his own, but
as high priest that year he prophesied that Jesus would
die for the Jewish nation, and not only for that nation
but also for the scattered children of God, to bring them
together and make them one.

JOHN 11:49–52

(John makes scant reference to the trial before the
high priest in 18:19–24. This prophecy was sufficient
to state the outcome.)

Mary anoints Jesus' feet

John 12:1–8 begins with John's account of Jesus'
anointing in Bethany by his friend Mary, whom we
have read about in the previous story. She pours a
pound of very expensive perfume to anoint his feet,
drying them with her hair. Meanwhile, Judas is outraged and speaks out against what he sees as waste,
but Jesus explains it as a pre-anointing for his burial.
This is not the only time in John that a man and a
woman are brought into sharp comparison to the
detriment of the former.

The plot is gathering pace and the intention now
is to kill Lazarus, who is, of course, a prime witness

(12:9–11). Jesus enters Jerusalem to great acclaim (12:12–19). The final piece in the puzzle seems to be the arrival of some Greeks to see Jesus. The Gentiles must be present to witness his lifting up, his glorification (12:20–36). This leads Jesus to explain the essential nature of his death, like a seed dying in the ground, in order to bring about new life. The 'hour has come' and he continues to teach the crowd, though they understandably struggle to comprehend his meaning.

The first half of the gospel of John draws to a close with a reflection on the faith or lack of faith which God's work will always encounter (12:36–43) and a summary of what Jesus has taught in the preceding chapters (12:44–50). These verses might be profitably used as a checklist, alongside 1:1–18, to see how this teaching has been acted out in the intervening chapters.

Now we are ready for the intense and somewhat claustrophobic atmosphere of the upper room, the trial and the final events of Jesus' life. This causes a huge change in atmosphere, telescoped as it is into a very short space of time.

The last supper and Jesus' farewell conversations (13:1—17:26)

These chapters of John clearly tell the story of Jesus' final meal with his disciples, familiar from the other gospels, but also introduce us to very unfamiliar aspects of that occasion. There is no eating together, no account of preparation; on the other hand we have the account of Jesus' washing the disciples' feet in chapter 13, three chapters of dialogue and discourses (chapters 14—16) which are absent in the other gospels and a final prayer of Jesus in chapter 17.

An overview of this section

These chapters might be divided up as follows:

- Washing the disciples' feet (13:1–17)
- The betrayal of Judas (13:18–30)
- The first dialogue between Jesus and his disciples (13:31—14:31)
- The parable of the vine (15:1–17)
- Jesus prepares his disciples for testing (15:18—16:4)
- The second dialogue between Jesus and his disciples (16:4–33)
- Jesus' final prayer (17:1–26)

Washing the disciples' feet

Chapter 13 marks a real change of gear in the overall narrative of John. Everything seems to slow down and become very focused. Jesus takes this opportunity to get up from the table, take off his outer garment and wrap a towel around his waist, and begins to wash the feet of his disciples. Simon Peter is outraged that his Lord should demean himself by assuming the task of a servant in that society. Jesus, however, insists that receiving this work is the essential prelude to being part of Jesus' company (13:6–11). Characteristically, Peter swings from passionate refusal to passionate and excessive embrace.

However, whenever water is around, it is almost certain that John intends to at least allude to further sacramental meaning. In a sense the washing is a kind of baptism, as Jesus embraces the whole of his followers with a single act of washing. Without this washing, they cannot be part of him (13:8). The Christian rite of baptism and its significance may well be in view.

The whole incident, so simple on the surface, as so often in John, is then interpreted (13:12–17). This act of deepest humility illustrates the condescension and commitment of the incarnation. It recalls the character of the servant of the Lord in Isaiah 40—55, who gives his life completely for the well-being of others. Throughout John, Jesus is completely aware of his status as God's Son and his divine origins, yet his servanthood is expressed in supreme acts of love, just as his greatest glorification is to hang in shame upon the cross. This example is not self-serving but points to how true disciples should behave (13:15–17).

'Now that I, your Lord and Teacher, have washed your feet, you also should wash one another's feet. I have set you an example that you should do as I have done for you.'
JOHN 13:14–15

The betrayal of Judas

Judas's betrayal hangs over the proceedings (13:18–30). As Judas takes the proffered morsel of bread, he commits himself to the act of betrayal and is lost. 'Satan entered into him' (13:27) and guides his future actions. Symbolically, he departs into the night (13:30).

The first dialogue between Jesus and his disciples

The first farewell dialogue between Jesus and his disciples now follows as Jesus seeks to prepare them for what is about to happen (13:31—14:31). This is a good moment for him to state his manifesto, his 'new command' of love (13:34–35), familiar to readers of the other gospels as Jesus' summary of the law (Mark 12:28–31): to love God and to love one's neighbour.

The structure of this dialogue is shaped by questions from four different disciples. First are Peter's questions, then Thomas', then Philip's and lastly Judas'.

Peter's questions and their answers concern Jesus' actual departure (13:36—14:4). He claims that, heroically, he would go anywhere with Jesus and receives the crushing prediction of his threefold denial of Jesus. Conversely, Jesus is going where he can prepare a place for all his followers and reassures them that they will know how to get there.

Thomas' question picks up where Jesus has left off and asks, 'How can we know the way?' (14:5–7). This provides the setting for another of the 'I am' sayings of John. Rather than being a geographical place or a set of specific rules or instructions for getting there, Jesus says, 'I am the way and the truth and the life. No one comes to the Father except through me' (14:6). The instruction is absolute and denies the existence of any other way to God, rather like the parable of the gate in 10:7–10 and assumed throughout John's gospel in the exalted and exclusive claims about Jesus.

Philip's question is a request to see the Father: that's all he's asking (14:8–21)! One can now sense Jesus' frustration. Have they not had enough experience of Jesus himself? His words? The signs he has performed? These should be sufficient in themselves to demonstrate who Jesus is. What's more, his followers will be empowered to live a similar life to his own. They only need to ask, receive the Holy Spirit and remain obedient to his word, *abiding* in him.

Finally, Judas' (not Iscariot) question seeks clarification as to how Jesus will reveal himself to his disciples but not to the world (14:22–24). Jesus' reply shifts the responsibility decisively from himself to those who see and hear him. Compare 3:17–21, where Jesus clarifies that he was not sent by the Father to condemn the world, but the world is self-condemned by its response to the light they are encountering. A response of faith and obedience is required.

Jesus closes this first discourse with a summary (14:25–31). He will send the Holy Spirit to teach them all that they will need. He blesses them with his peace to see them through all the difficult times ahead. His departure is in obedience to the Father, so they have no need to be anxious.

The parable of the vine

In 15:1–17, Jesus tells the parable of the vine, which explores the theme which we have seen before – that Jesus' followers must remain in him. The picture language is taken very obviously from Isaiah's illustration about Israel as a vine (Isaiah 5:1–7). The vine is Israel, and we are told that God planted this special vineyard which he really loved. He took every step to make sure it could flourish and do well. It was well watered and protected and tended. Unfortunately, it yielded only wild and inedible grapes, so God resolved to abandon it to its fate. It will become a wasteland.

The background of divine judgement cannot be ignored in a gospel that so persistently presents Jesus as the fulfilment of Israel's destiny. Now, Jesus assumes the mantel of being the vine; Isaiah's image of the vineyard has been reduced to that of a single vine, namely Jesus, with the disciples as branches.

The theme of 'remaining', 'abiding' and 'staying', which we have observed frequently throughout the gospel, reaches its peak as Jesus likens his followers to the branches of a vine. When the branches are attached to the vine, they will be fruitful, as God had wished for his original vineyard, Israel. The fruit envisaged here is that they should love each other with a totality similar to Jesus' own love for the world (15:12–17).

However, if they fail to stay attached to the vine (to 'remain', 'abide'), they will be pruned and burnt – a clear image of divine judgement. There is no suggestion that such branches might somehow be grafted back into the vine after they have been pruned away.

'I am the vine; you are the branches. If you remain in me and I in you, you will bear much fruit; apart from me you can do nothing.'
JOHN 15:5

Who is the *Paraclete*?

In these farewell conversations, Jesus' main aim seems to be to encourage and teach his disciples, especially concerning the Holy Spirit, often referred to here as the *Paraclete* (translated variously as 'Comforter', 'Counsellor', 'Advocate' and 'Helper' in

14:16, 26; 15:26; 16:7). In 14:16, he is described as 'another *Paraclete*', employing the Greek term which implies 'another of the same sort' rather than being different in any way. As Jesus is about to ascend to the Father and effectively no longer be physically with them, his Spirit/*Paraclete* will come alongside them, continuing the ministry of Jesus.

He will show them the things of Christ; he will teach them things to come and everything else that they need to know; he will assist their memories of past teaching and bear witness to Christ; it is he who will dwell in them and they will do 'greater works' even than those of Christ, presumably in total rather than each as individuals.

'If you love me, keep my commands. And I will ask the Father, and he will give you another advocate to help you and be with you forever – the Spirit of truth.'
JOHN 14:15–17

This description of the nature and work of the Holy Spirit is unique to John and significantly fills out our understanding of him.

Jesus prepares his discples for testing

The various threats to the life of the early Christian community are clearly laid out in John 15:18—16:4. They will be hated and persecuted just as Jesus was (18:18–25). It is a sign that their persecutors really hate God the Father. More specifically, there will be a systematic ejection from their synagogues, which we first encountered in the story of the man born blind in chapter 9. But the first readers of the gospel must have been very conscious of this activity as their present experience. The link back to the life and teaching of Jesus is very strong.

The second dialogue between Jesus and his disciples

In many ways, John 16:4–33 resembles a review of some of the themes first aired in 13:31—14:31, so it can be helpful to think of these verses as the second of Jesus' dialogues with the disciples.

Jesus begins by recalling the anxiety that they have already expressed concerning his departure. In fact, he says, it is for their own good since only then will the *Paraclete* come, who will judge the world and prove that the world was wrong all along. The Spirit will lead them further into aspects of the truth that Jesus could never have conferred during his life upon earth. There will be continuity with Jesus' earthly ministry, but the *Paraclete* will clearly reign over the life of Jesus' followers, inspiring them, when they are obedient, into all truth.

'But the Advocate, the Holy Spirit, whom the Father will send in my name, will teach you all things and will remind you of everything that I have said to you.'
JOHN 14:26

The disciples interject that they do not really understand Jesus' words about seeing him again after a 'little while'. This uncertainty about the return of Christ has exercised the church ever since. For these disciples, it could simply refer to those days following the resurrection when Jesus blessed them with his teaching and presence. It could also refer to his return in the person of the Holy Spirit, though that seems a little less likely. But there is also the possibility that Jesus' second coming, still future, may be in view.

Somewhat surprisingly, the disciples say they now understand (16:29–30). Jesus affirms them in that!

Jesus' final prayer

Chapter 17 offers us a version of what the other gospels recall as the garden of Gethsemane (see Mark 14:32–42). Gone is the location and the accompanying disciples, but we witness Jesus praying a climactic prayer prior to his arrest. Realising that the end is near, he prays that God the Father will be glorified in all that happens (17:1–5). Consequently, he also prays for himself – that he might be glorified.

Next, he prays for his disciples. He tells the Father how they belong to him and that they have obeyed his words (17:6–19). They will carry the mantel of the mission that Jesus is about to lay down. He prays for their experience of a joy like that which Jesus experienced – a joy which would be expressed in the world itself, since they are not to taken out of it but were to remain there as Jesus' witnesses.

Finally, Jesus prays for all of those who come to faith because of their ministry (17:20–26). The relationship between Jesus, the Father and all his future followers, by the power of the Holy Spirit, is often referred to by the term 'coinherence', which is best defined by these seemingly mystical verses:

'I ask not only on behalf of these, but also on behalf of those who will believe in me through their word, that they may all be one. As you, Father, are in me and I am in you, may they also be in us, so that the world may believe that you have sent me… I in them and you in me, that they may become completely one.'

JOHN 17:20–21, 23

The betrayal, arrest, trial, crucifixion and burial (18:1—19:42)

The betrayal and arrest

Jesus is arrested, having been identified by the kiss of Judas, as predicted (18:1–11). The manner of the arrest underlies an often-repeated assertion that, in John, Jesus hardly seems to be human at all. At the arrest, the armed guards and crowd are hugely fearful and intimidated. Jesus, on the other hand, is completely in control. We must take this seriously.

Man or superman?

It is a commonly heard view that, in John, Jesus seems at best always in control of events and almost 'Olympian' in his detachment; at worst, readers sometimes say they cannot relate to him because of this. One friend of mine once commented that Jesus, in John, 'always seems to be walking about three feet above the ground'. I could see her point.

Jesus, as we read about him in John, rarely seems perturbed by anything. He seems completely in control of his circumstances, knows absolutely everything and is aware that he is God's Son. Even when arrested, tried and crucified, he displays very little concern, walking through the pages of the gospel with not a care in the world!

This is only part of the story and there are two major things wrong with this opinion. First, in John, Jesus displays a great many human emotions and characteristics. He has very human conversations, engaging warmly with other people (for example, chapters 3, 4 and 9). He sometimes seems to despair of his followers but kindly cares for them (chapters 14—16). He expresses great anger (chapter 8). He is hugely affectionate, even to the point of weeping at Lazarus' death (chapter 11). He cares for his mother at the cross (chapter 19).

Second, it may well be that it is the circumstances of writing that foster this perception of gloriously 'walking three feet above the ground'. John may be reflecting the understanding at the time of writing, when Jesus' identity as risen Lord, rather than his humanity, dominated the church's perception of him. A few years later, very many mosaics and icons would depict him in heavenly glory and not as the human carpenter of Nazareth. The critical setting of hostility between Jewish believers and unbelievers may have caused the evangelist to emphasise certain divine aspects of Jesus' character rather than more human traits.

The trial

As in the other gospels, there is a Jewish trial and a Roman trial. First comes the trial before Annas (18:12–28). Compared with the account in the other gospel, this Jewish trial is not very detailed and, apart from pointing out that he has always acted very publicly and being slapped across the face for his pains, nothing very new happens. In the midst of this activity is John's account of Peter's three incidents of denial. What follows now is the much more dramatic trial before Pilate.

The Jews give themselves away completely as they hand Jesus over to Pilate (18:29–32). It was always their intention to get him executed, but they had no authority to do so (18:31). Pilate, of course, is completely out of his depth and, although he is nominally the most powerful man in Judea, he does not know how to exercise his power, nor how to cope with this holy man who is so hated by so many people.

The dialogue between Jesus and Pilate focuses around the topic of who is in charge. 'Are you the King of the Jews?' he asks (18:33), only to learn that Jesus rules a very different kind of kingdom than what Pilate is used to. Typical politician that he is, he asks, 'What is truth?' He really doesn't know, though the reader is aware that in front of him stands the one who is actually 'the way and the truth and the life' (14:6) and who is 'full of grace and truth' (1:14). The whole scene is a wonderful example of John's ironic way of storytelling.

Further irony ensues when the crowd reject their real King and opt to release a bandit (18:39–40). And that very King is mockingly dressed up in kingly kit: a purple robe and a crown (of thorns). A further irony occurs when Pilate presents him to the crowd, not just in mock-kingly form, but saying, 'Here is the man!' (19:5). Is he just a man, or *the* man? Might he be the Son of Man, seen by the prophet in Daniel

7:13–14? Or is he a sort of second Adam seen in the garden after the resurrection by Mary (20:15)?

Pilate is puzzled and distracted and raises once again the question of Jesus' origins (19:9). But Jesus declines to answer, drawing from Pilate a bullying assertion of his authority to have him crucified. Jesus reminds him that all authority is ultimately God's. The Jews, meanwhile, play their trump card, which must have scared Pilate greatly, namely, that to let this pretender go free would demonstrate that he, Pilate, was no friend of Caesar's. It is only a matter of time until Pilate takes this charge seriously and hands Jesus over, hoping to get rid of him.

There is one crowning irony, as Pilate sits Jesus on the judgement seat (19:13) and proclaims, 'Here is your King.' The same declaration adorns the notice fixed above Jesus' head as he is crucified, to the intense irritation of the Jews! But, ironically again, Pilate asserts the authority of the written word (19:22).

Pilate had a notice prepared and fastened to the cross. It read: JESUS OF NAZARETH, THE KING OF THE JEWS… and the sign was written in Aramaic, Latin and Greek.
JOHN 19:19–20

The crucifixion

The scene closes with Jesus, just before his death, delivering his mother to the care of the disciple whom he loved, the beloved disciple.

Throughout the whole account, great care is taken to point out the fulfilment of scripture. First, the soldiers decide not to tear his clothing (19:23–24; see Psalm 22:18), then Jesus expresses his thirst (19:28–30; see Psalm 22:15), then he is the one whose legs are not broken (19:31–36; see Exodus 12:46; Numbers 9:12; Psalm 34:20) but his body is pierced with a spear (19:34–37; see Zechariah 12:10).

The burial

Following his death, the burial rehearses again the extravagant behaviour of God and of those who love him. Earlier extravagance is seen with wine at the wedding feast at Cana (2:1–11), the abundance of food at the feeding of the five thousand (6:1–15) and Mary of Bethany's anointing with perfume (12:1–11). Now, Nicodemus, accompanying Joseph of Arimathea, brings about 75 pounds of myrrh and aloes to anoint the body of Jesus – an extraordinary and unnecessary amount, reflecting his devotion and love. But can anything be too great for this man, Jesus? Whether this is evidence of Nicodemus having come to a place of faith or just an example of extreme affection is open to interpretation. John leaves us to decide for ourselves.

The resurrection of Jesus (20)

The 'first day of the week' is the day of resurrection, which is why Christians worship then and not on Saturday, the sabbath proper. It is the day of new creation. Simon Peter and the 'other disciple' run to the tomb following the initial report of Mary Magdalene (20:1–9). The other disciple not only saw what was there but also converted this raw experience into faith (20:8), though clearly there were still things they were unable to square with scripture and their own understanding of life.

As the two men go home to resume normal life in some way, Mary Magdalene remains (that word again!) and is rewarded with the most wonderful encounter with the risen Lord (20:10–18). When she mistakes him for the gardener, John intends us to make a link with the first gardener, Adam, and the garden of Eden, which represent the first creation. Jesus represents the new or second creation. In

Paul's terms, he is the second Adam (Romans 5:12–21; 1 Corinthians 15:21–22, 45–49).

Mary Magdalene went to the disciples with the news: 'I have seen the Lord!'
JOHN 20:18

Jesus appears next to all his disciples apart from Thomas (20:19–23). He twice proclaims peace to them, shows them his wounds and breathes out the Holy Spirit upon them, conferring the authority to forgive sin.

Again Jesus said, 'Peace be with you! As the Father has sent me, I am sending you.' And with that he breathed on them and said, 'Receive the Holy Spirit.'
JOHN 20:21–22

Thomas, 'the Twin', is unfortunately known to us principally on account of his doubting the truth of the resurrection. But his expression of doubt affords us the great proof of the physicality of the resurrection (20:24–29). Doubting Thomas is invited to look and physically examine those wounds, declaring, as the climax of the whole gospel, 'My Lord and my God' (20:28).

In a very real sense, chapter 20 closes the gospel of John (20:30–31). These verses have all the appearance of summing up the purpose of John: he has assembled a great many sign(posts) to enable his readers to believe and have life. It is a selection from the many stories he could have used and which he clearly knew of. Like all the gospel writers, he chooses what to tell us and has a purpose throughout, which we can discover if we read his gospel carefully.

The epilogue (21)

It is curious that, having apparently closed his narrative with chapter 20, John should take a deep metaphorical breath to tell us of Jesus' encounter by the lake with a few disciples, but especially Simon Peter and the disciple whom he loved.

The setting resembles very closely the calling of the first disciples by the lake (Luke 5:1–11), when Jesus uses their boat to give himself space to preach to the crowd. On this occasion, as in the earlier one, the fishermen have had a fruitless night on the lake. Jesus instructs them to throw out their net again to haul in 153 fish (21:1–14). This is a mysterious and even gratuitous number, which has spawned many different interpretations, though the most likely one is that any professional fishermen would be in the habit of carefully counting every fish to share out the spoils of their efforts. The beloved disciple recognises the Lord's work.

And in another partial re-enactment (this time of the feeding of the five thousand), Jesus feeds them with bread and fish. This also demonstrates the physicality of his resurrection.

Finally, in the most beautiful scene of restoration, Jesus omits even to mention Peter's threefold denial of him, let alone attribute blame, but asks him three times if he loves him (21:15–19). Bound up with that is a re-commissioning to 'feed my sheep'. This sets the template for Peter's future ministry and, in a final scene, he is instructed by Jesus that a knowledge of his own future ministry does not mean that he will necessarily be informed as to the future of the beloved disciple.

Again Jesus said, 'Simon son of John, do you love me?'
JOHN 21:16

John ends with testimony as to the source of his story (21:24–25). This does not identify the writer of this gospel but does insist that eyewitness testimony lies behind it. The 'we' of verse 24 suggests the possibility that several hands were involved in the process of bringing this gospel to its present form.

6

John and other New Testament writings

John and the other gospels

The most obvious point of comparison is with the other three gospels, Matthew, Mark and Luke. These are usually referred to as the Synoptic gospels, signifying that they are looking at the life of Jesus from one particular angle and resemble each other essentially in style, substance and presentation. John is also telling the same story, but so much is different. While scholars tend to argue in favour of some form of literary relationship between Matthew, Mark and Luke (in some way they have copied from each other), almost no one nowadays suggests the same thing about John. Here are some of the ways in which John is different:

- The content of the stories is so different. A great many of John's stories and teaching only appear there, and much that is in the Synoptic gospels is absent from John. For example, the stories of the wedding, the woman at the well, the healing of the blind man and the raising of Lazarus are unique. He omits any birth or infancy stories, most of the healing miracles and the ascension into heaven.

- John introduces the theme of Jesus' kingship, but the classic teaching about the kingdom of God, found throughout the other gospels, is almost completely absent. Instead, where you might expect there to be such teaching he includes teaching about 'eternal life'. There is no sermon on the mount nor the Lord's Prayer.

- John does not present Jesus as a storyteller, and there are hardly any parables.

- He all but omits the last supper or, at least, relates it so obliquely that no institution of bread and wine ever occurs.

Whether it is John the witness or Jesus himself or the gospel narrator speaking, the style is fairly uniform. Jesus doesn't speak in many parables, nor does he deliver the pithy and wise one-liners that we are familiar with from the Synoptic gospels. Instead, he tends to speak in long, ruminative discourses.

Since John is very different, does that mean he is unhistorical and making it all up? That has been the view of some who assume on other grounds that the other gospels are more to be relied upon for historical detail. However, what is more likely is that John's gospel is a distinctive selection of teaching, chosen for particular ends. His approach is much more highly thought-through and represents his own thinking and reflection to the point that the words and actions of Jesus come out in his own idiosyncratic way.

John and the Old Testament

The idea of Jesus as the *Logos* (Word) in the first verse of the gospel has led some to think that, here and elsewhere, John is using ideas from the Greek (Hellenistic) world to explore the gospel. The Old Testament is more significant, however, in understanding John's gospel. John directly quotes the Old Testament 14 times and is concerned, as are the other gospels, with the way in which Jesus fulfils the Old Testament scripture. There are many other allusions to the Old Testament, including references to Abraham and Moses, the provision of manna in the wilderness, Israel as a vine and the image of the good shepherd. Details of his crucifixion echo details of the Passover meal.

As Jesus said in rebuking the Jewish leaders, 'You study the Scriptures diligently because you think that in them you have eternal life. These are the very Scriptures that testify about me, yet you refuse to come to me to have life' (5:38–40).

The rest of the New Testament

John is often assumed to be the last written of all the New Testament writings because of its very developed theology and its extremely high theology of the person of Christ. However, development and sophistication are not always a sign of a later date.

It is quite likely that the author of John's gospel also wrote the epistles of John, because the style is so similar and there are lots of similarities of themes. Conversely, the style and content of Revelation are so different from both the gospel and the epistles that it is unlikely that the same John wrote it (even though the author identifies himself as 'John' in Revelation 1:9). Some have argued, however, that the style of Revelation is deliberately challenging to reflect just how difficult it is to express heavenly truths in human language. If that is the case, John the apostle might still be responsible for writing it.

7

John's continuing message

Main themes

What we can say is that John offers us a very exalted portrait of Jesus – what is often described as a very high Christology. He also implicitly covers many other areas of teaching such as the relationships within the Trinity, which is not articulated as such, but the foundations are securely there. There is a full discussion of the Fatherhood of God and the person of the Holy Spirit.

John also has his distinctive presentation of the cross – which is not in conflict with other viewpoints – which doesn't just focus on Jesus as the lamb of God, but presents the cross as the ultimate point of divine revelation and the place of divine enthronement.

John has a profound theology of mission, beginning with the Samaritan woman in John 4 and climaxing in his account of the great commission in John 20:21–23.

He does not give much teaching on ethical or moral behaviour but focuses upon the essential relationship between the believer and Christ through the Holy Spirit.

How should we teach and preach from John today?

Preachers often try to preach from John in the kind of linear way they might use for Paul's epistles – starting at the beginning and tackling the gospel section by section. But this does not work well, because John's stories and discourses are so long and integrated, and it is hard to keep the thread clear from week to week.

There are three approaches to preaching from John that might work better. The first would be to take smaller passages – for instance, a five- or six-week sermon series on 'the bread of life', exploring chapter six. This approach has often been used successfully with all or parts of the farewell discourse in chapters 14—16.

Secondly, the preacher could focus on John's key themes, tracing John's treatment of them through the gospel – for instance, glory, faith, light or the festivals. Studies on John's characters might fit into this category.

Thirdly – perhaps more difficult but certainly worth trying – I would encourage preachers simply to immerse themselves in John's very special atmosphere, trying to feel his approach and concerns from the inside. What makes this gospel 'tick'? Why does John start the gospel as he does, and portray Jesus as he does? Why are people so divided in their responses to Jesus? Why are 'the Jews' so opposed to him? Who were these 'Jews', and how can we make sense of their attitudes for today's sensitivities?

Finally, reading John's gospel with others in a small group over several weeks is a very enriching experience as together you notice, explore and engage with the detail and depth of John's message.

Further reading

Andreas J. Köstenberger, *Encountering John*
  (Baker Academic, 1999)

Colin Kruse, *John*
  (Tyndale New Testament Commentaries)
  (IVP, 2017)

Andrew Lincoln, *John*
  (Black's New Testament Commentaries)
  (Black's, 2006)

Robert Willoughby and Elaine Carr, *What's God Like?*
  John's gospel
  (Bible Max: More Time with God)
  (Scripture Union, 2007)

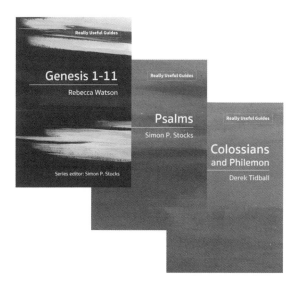

Get to grips with the Bible with these exceptionally useful short guides! Each Really Useful Guide focuses on a specific biblical book, making it come to life for the reader, enabling them to understand the message and to apply its truth to today's circumstances. Though not a commentary, it gives valuable insight into the book's message. Though not an introduction, it summarises the important aspects of the book to aid reading and application.

Really Useful Guides

brfonline.org.uk/collections/really-useful-guides

BRF

Transforming
lives and communities

Christian growth and understanding of the Bible

Resourcing individuals, groups and leaders in churches for their own spiritual journey and for their ministry

Church outreach in the local community

Offering two programmes that churches are embracing to great effect as they seek to engage with their local communities and transform lives

Teaching Christianity in primary schools

Working with children and teachers to explore Christianity creatively and confidently

Children's and family ministry

Working with churches and families to explore Christianity creatively and bring the Bible alive **parenting for faith**

Visit **brf.org.uk** for more information on BRF's work

brf.org.uk